8 Steps to Freedom

+

Answers to Life's Toughest Questions

Judy Winkler

8 Steps to Freedom
+
Answers to Life's Toughest Questions

Copyright @ 2013

8 Steps to Freedom may be purchased through book dealers and on line book stores, www.SacredLife.com, and Judy Winkler's website: www.coachjudywinkler.com

ISBN: 978-09728592-5-7
ISBN: 097285925X
Library of Congress Control Number: 2013934433

The information, ideas, and suggestions in this book are not intended as a substitute for professional advice. Before following any suggestions contained in this book, consult your physician or mental health professional. Neither the authors nor the publisher shall be liable or responsible for any loss or damage allegedly arising as a consequence of your use or application of any information or suggestions in this book.

Cover Design by: Samuel Rivera www.samriveradesign.com, and Daniel Young.

Sacred Life Publishers™
www.SacredLife.com
Printed in the United States of America

Dedicated to

my grandchildren,

Daniel Young,

Joshua Young

and

Kendra Van Valkenburgh

Contents

Preface

The 8 steps to freedom are in fact 8 powerful tools designed to permanently and effectively change thinking and behavior.

Behavior will change as soon as the thoughts that fuel the behavior changes. When concepts of self-control, self-awareness, and self-mastery are cultivated and embraced, amazing shifts occur. Using the tools or processes offered in this book will absolutely change the quality of your experiences.

My goal is to help every reader lead a productive and joyful life. Applying the tools in this book, *8 Steps to Freedom* is a ticket to success.

Throughout this book, you may see the word, God. Please substitute the image, energy or word that feels most comfortable for you – Jesus, Buddha, Spirit, Allah, Higher Self, whatever word you use to signify the eternal, loving energy, presence that dwells within you and around you.

May this be the life-changing experience you dreamed of to step into the person you were born to be.

My blessings to you for your courage and willingness to dare to change.

Namaste! (The God in me salutes the God in you.)

Freedom Begins . . .

Freedom begins with new tools

When I was in the first grade, I was jealous of rich kids because they had advantages I didn't have. They seemed to glide through life with ease. They bragged about going to plays, fancy parties and fun places. They spoke beautifully, did the right things, and knew about life. They had music and dance lessons, travel experiences, and they got to wear new, beautiful clothes.

The difference between those rich kids and me was that they were given excellent tools to get through life.

I desperately needed tools to make school and life easier. Since I was dyslectic, I felt cursed and stupid because I could barely read. Arithmetic made no sense and my language skills were so poor, I was ashamed to speak. I felt ugly because I wore second hand clothes and in general, I felt unacceptable.

Growing up, did you have excellent tools? Would life have been easier if you were better prepared?

So what are tools?

Think of it this way: A gourmet cook couldn't produce delicious meals if her only tool was a wooden spoon. A master painter couldn't produce without a canvas or paint. If your only tool was a jack hammer and needed to replace a light bulb, your tool wouldn't work well, right? It makes perfect sense that we can only use the tools we have – even if ineffective. To produce the best work and to make life easy and fun, we need good tools.

So the difference between you and others are your tools.

For instance, if you were given superior communication tools, you would probably get what you wanted. Here is an example of a communication tool:

Poor Tool: Open the door right now!

Effective Tool: My arms are full; will you please open the door?

Which example would make both people feel good about the encounter?

If a gardener only had a pair of scissors to cut the lawn, he would get on his hands and knees to trim the grass. If he had a power mower to ride, he'd do things differently. Without excellent tools, we will keep doing the same things over and over and get the same results.

We don't know what we don't know. In other words, we don't know different ways of thinking, acting or being until we are shown. I'm always surprised when I visit other people's homes to see how differently they live. Recently I visited a friend who stores lettuce in a different way. After washing and drying it, he wraps the lettuce in a cloth towel and stores it in the refrigerator. I tried this new way and it keeps lettuce fresh for a few days. I learned a new tool.

Learning and using new tools makes life easier and much more fun. We each want an easier and more joyful life, yes?

So, it isn't that rich people are better; they had better tools. You will see your life change the moment you learn to use new tools.

A new tool changed my life when I was 17 years old. At 16, I ran away from home. I worked as a live-in maid and nanny, then entered college. In my first semester, I sat in the front row of class. A handsome, young professor walked out in a tweed jacket with suede arm patches. He stood before me in a Superman pose and said 16 words that changed me. He said, "The way you take this class is the way you take life, so watch and learn."

Until that moment, I had never observed my thoughts, emotions or my actions. I never paid attention to what I was thinking or what I was doing. Hearing these 16 words felt like a bucket of ice water waking me from a deep sleep.

Never before had I observed that I was an arrogant, yet scared teenager. I had never noticed that I used most of my energy trying to look smart and witty, and superior, (even though it was an act). I saw that I spent most of my energy keeping myself safe from being hurt or overpowered by anyone – particularly men.

For the first time in my life, I observed my thoughts, noticed what I felt and what I said. This was my first experience of telling myself the truth about me.

So, now that I knew the truth, what could I do about it?

I needed to learn tools to help make my life easier. It took years to find tools and processes and refine them. Now I'll share them with you. You are getting the best of my search and experience.

Are you ready for some new tools?

FIRST TOOL: The Power of Now

This tool identifies where your mind is. When you bring yourself to the present moment, you are most likely to make the best decisions and act from a place of freedom and power.

I'm going to ask you to use your imagination.

Imagine on the wall in front of you is a four-foot circle like a giant clock or directional compass. Instead of numbers or north, south, east and west, there are four words. The top says **Future.** The bottom says **Past.** The left side says **Me** and the right side says **You.**

Pretend you take the circle off the wall and place it under your feet so you are standing in the center of the circle called Now. This Now circle you are standing on represents the present moment, which includes the power of God. I believe there is a life energy that moves through us, that is greater than we are, and is universal power. I call it God, but you can decide on a word you like that represents this power.

Using your imagination, think of yesterday and something you ate. Because you are telling yourself a story about something that has already happened, take a physical step backward onto the spot called **Past.** Now step back into the center of Now.

Think of something you will do tomorrow or next week or something you are worried about and take a step forward onto the spot called **Future.** Then step back into the center of Now.

Now think about someone you are judging or blaming – it might be the long line you had to stand in, it might be paying taxes, the economy, the government, a co-worker, or a noisy neighbor who bugs you. Take a physical step to your right into the **You** position. Step back into the center of Now.

Imagine a time when you felt like a victim, (I call it "poor pitiful me"), or when you were bullying yourself, thinking things that were bad or wrong about you. Now think of a time when you played "I'm the hero in my world." I'm so wonderful and perfect that no one could possibly be this great. Physically step to the left into the **Me** spot. This spot can represent both a victim posture as well as a grandiose posture. The common denominator is the word "Me." Step back into the center of Now.

Let's imagine you have this invisible circle underneath you all the time. You become aware of your thoughts - especially when you have an emotional reaction or get stuck. With this tool, you can identify if your thoughts and emotions are in the past, the future, blaming someone else, blaming yourself or being full of yourself. You cannot make a clear decision, take action or change your feelings or circumstance until you step back into the middle circle of Now, which represents this current moment in time.

The Now spot is the only point of power. Can you see how you can get distracted and get stuck in the past, the future, blaming or judging someone else or yourself?

The present moment is where we can access the wisdom and power of God to make choices, take clear action and solve problems. The Now circle is the best place to be if you want freedom.

To stay in the present moment, continually ask yourself where you are on the circle – the past, future, blame or in the present moment? The questions, "How do I feel and what do I need?" keep us present so we can make our best choices and decisions. This imaginary circle will keep you powerful because you'll operate from the present moment using God's power.

When I need a *fast trip* back to the present, I put my hands in front of me, palms facing each other (as if I were saying, "The fish was this big!") The space between my two palms is the present moment. Everything else is the past or future.

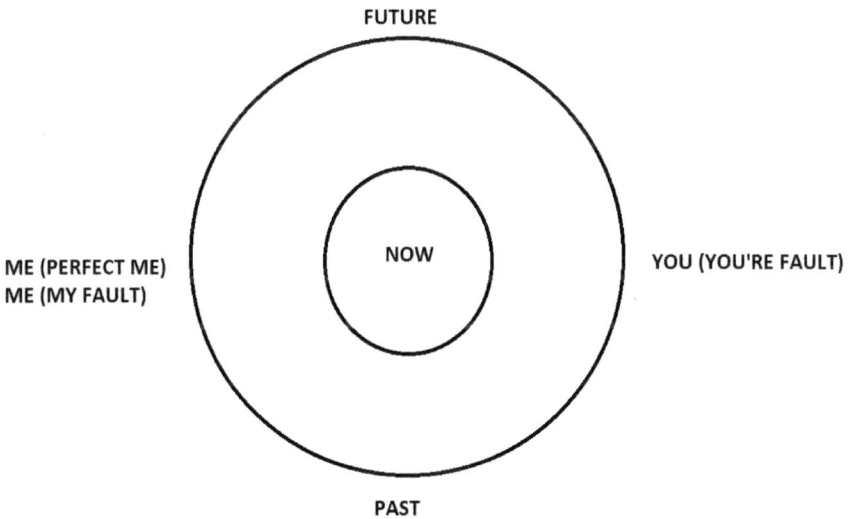

FUTURE

ME (PERFECT ME)
ME (MY FAULT)

NOW

YOU (YOU'RE FAULT)

PAST

SECOND TOOL – The Four Agreements
based on Miguel Ruiz's book, *The Four Agreements*

Stay in integrity

A client asked me to define the word integrity. I told him it was doing the right thing for the right reason, all the time – even when no one is looking. It means keeping your word, being honest, truthful, reliable, upright, and being your best self. If you are a person of integrity, doors open because others trust you.

I heard a story that happened in the early 1900's; a wealthy man in New York was known as a man of integrity. A *most* expensive piece of property became available. Multiple investors showed up with lines of credit from their banks, their lawyers, and contracts but the seller chose to sell to this man simply on a handshake with no contract, no attorney because this was a man of his word.

We've all heard stories of trustworthy people being highly rewarded with gifts, opportunities, and respect.

Don't take things personally

It is most common to get your feelings hurt or think someone else's upset is about you. *It isn't about You!* Kids think that every upset in their family is their fault. Adults frequently carry the belief that everyone's upset has to do with them or everything is their fault, they caused the problem, etc. Here is the truth: You cannot make anyone upset. It is their choice. They may not like what you said or did, but it is their choice to react in either an unpleasant way or respond in a pleasant way.

11

What am I saying? If we are standing in line and you step on my toe. I can choose to scream and hit you or I can simply say, "Ouch! You are on my toe." It is my choice. Conversely, if I accidentally step on your foot, I'm not trying to get even with you or hurt you, I simply lost my balance. It was an accident. Don't make everything about you.

Road rage is a perfect example of taking the actions of another personally. A man is driving his car at a normal speed. A driver in a pick-up behind him spilled coffee on himself, his boss just called to warn him to get into work now or he's fired. The pick-up driver is stressed and beeps his horn repeatedly at the car driving at a normal speed.

He keeps beeping, then finally speeds around him, yells out the window and gives a one-finger salute. This leads us to the next agreement.

Don't assume anything

The road rage story can escalate to the higher level if the driver in the car takes the horn beeping personally and thinks the pick-up truck driver is trying to get him mad. If he reacts by assuming it is a personal gesture of anger, it could end up in a traffic fatality.

Another example of assuming things is silence. When someone doesn't talk to you or doesn't call you when you expect him to, you may assume they don't like you or that you've done something wrong. You don't know the story, so you make up one. We humans have a unique ability to rationalize or try to make sense of anything we do not know or understand. When we assume something, it indicates that we have not gathered the facts. Since we are uncomfortable not knowing, we make up something. When we get worried, we usually think the worst. It is wise to check things out – have the hard conversations to be sure you know what the real story is.

If you are having a conversation and someone suddenly looks sad or upset, don't assume you said or did anything. Check it out. For example, say, "Your expression changed; are you sad or upset?" That is much simpler than assuming what you do not know. It may be they have a pain in their side or someone walked by who looked like their grandmother who just died. We do NOT know unless we ask or are told. Don't assume. Don't tell yourself a story. Check out the facts by asking.

Many years ago, I was swept off my feet by a man. I wanted our relationship to unfold and grow into something long term. He wanted to become closer before I was ready. When I told him I was not ready for intimacy, he immediately dumped me. I was shocked and bummed. My girlfriend, Dottie did not assume anything. She asked the most probing questions that helped me unravel my jumbled feelings. She asked questions such as,

1. Are you disappointed because you thought this was going to be permanent?

2. Are you upset because he did not give you any warning?

3. Are you sad because he seemed like such a good partner?

4. Are you worried you will have to explain this to your friends and family?

She didn't assume she knew what was going on with me and checked it out. Her questions clarified my feelings too.

I heard about a woman who loved dogs. Her new apartment only allowed cats so she got a cat. The landlord stopped by after a few weeks to ask how things were going with her new cat. The woman said, "That damned cat won't fetch a ball, won't come when you call, he scratches furniture, jumps up on everything and even walks all over the kitchen counter!" She assumed the cat would act like a dog!

We have a picture of how things should look, how others should behave, how situations should unfold. These expectations only cause disappointment. See if you can accept how people and situations are. Accept what is and have no investment in the outcome. Don't expect a cat to be a dog. Tell another story – one of acceptance and gratitude for things as they are right now.

Always do your best

The fourth agreement is always do your best. Your best may look different than you thought. If you have invited guests for dinner and you get the flu, your best may not be 10 gourmet dishes that require days of preparation. Your best may be delivered pizza and salad, or a big pot of spaghetti. It may not be what you wanted or planned, but your best for that moment is all you can do.

I love the story of the Zen monk who was asked what he did *before* he was enlightened. He responded, "I chopped wood and carried water. When asked what he did *after* he was enlightened, he responded, "I chopped wood and carried water."

Think of each task that you do, big or small, simple or complicated, as a gift you are giving back into life. Make it your best.

THIRD TOOL – Calm and De-Stress Yourself

BREATHE.

Changing your breathing pattern is the fastest way to soothe yourself. I'll show you four different types of breathing tools. You decide which ones work best for you.

You might think, what a silly thing, everybody knows how to breathe. Did you know when we get upset, scared, or frustrated, we take shallow breaths? Shallow breaths do NOT fuel the brain completely so when the brain is not fueled, we can't think clearly. No wonder we get confused when we are scared or upset. Deep breaths not only help us use our brain power, they alter our physical and mental states.

As we go through the five breath tools to calm and soothe yourself, think about where you tend to get stressed, or stuck. Try a few different breathing techniques when you start to feel stress. One will suit the situation perfectly.

A. Belly breath

Sit up tall so your lungs have adequate space to move. Place both feet on the floor. Place the palm of one hand over your belly button and take in a deep, deep breath through your nose so you belly pushes your hand outward. Exhale through your mouth and notice when you fully exhale, your hand moves toward your backbone.

Let's try that now. Take a deep breath in through your nose, deep into your belly. Hold it a moment and exhale fully through your mouth so no air remains in your lungs.

Again - take another deep breath in through your nose, hold it a moment and exhale through the mouth. Did you notice your hand move?

I suggest you take five to seven deep breaths to stabilize yourself to feel balanced.

B. Darth Vader breath

Remember the Star Wars movie when Darth Vader was near, you could hear him breathe? Take a deep belly breath in, (just like you learned), but this time, exhale through the mouth partially closing your throat and exhale with a long "heh" sound.

Let's try that together. Deep breath in through the nose, partially close the throat and exhale fully with a long "heh" sound. Good.

Again. take five to seven deep breaths to get re-balanced.

C. Nose Toggle

Another breath tool is the nose toggle. This is a great tool one to use when you can't seem to clear your mind of what I call "the drunken monkeys." You know those times when your mind is filled with constant, nonsensical chatter? Concentrating on the nose toggle breath will distract the mind chatter to help you focus.

Here is how the nose toggle works. Place your thumb and index finger like a clothespin on your nose. Instead of pinching both nostrils, pretend your nose is a toggle switch that you turn on and off by moving it side to side. You close one side then the other to a count of four.

16

Let's try that together. Put your thumb and index finger in a position to pinch your nose. Instead, press the left nostril shut and breathe in deeply through the right nostril to the count of four. Then toggle over and press the right nostril shut and exhale through the left nostril, counting to four. Now breathe in through your right nostril, counting to four. Toggle over and open the left nostril and breathe out counting to four. Do this 5 times.

You can see how useful this breathing tool is when you want to stop the mind chatter and focus because it requires concentration to count to four while toggling back and forth and breathing in and out.

D. Laughter Yoga breath

This breath tool is used to shift your mood. It's guaranteed to cheer you up. Stand up with your hands on your hips and take a deep breath in through your nose, then as you exhale, slowly bend forward at the waist and loudly shout, "Ha, ha, ha, ha, ha."

Let's do it together. Stand with your hands on your hips, take a deep breath in through the nose. Exhale as you bend forward "ha, ha, ha, ha, ha." Good. Repeat five times and notice how cheerful you feel.

Can you see how these breath tools might be useful to you? When you get stuck, take a moment to change your breathing – choose one of the breath tools to bring oxygen to your brain and to re-balance yourself. If one breathing tool doesn't work well, try another. One is sure to help you.

Other Tools for Stress

Stress is part of life. Those of us who grew up with few coping tools, haven't learned to soothe ourselves. Without coping tools to de-stress, we remain anxiety-ridden. We become experts at worrying, being hyper-vigilant, staying geared up waiting for something horrible to happen. Some develop sleep disorders, ulcers, high blood pressure –you name it. To keep from going crazy, we create another reality (our own little world); we zone out, or medicate so we don't feel anything. You're not the Lone Ranger; we all do it to cope the best we can.

Whatever we practice for a long time, we get really good at whether it is worrying, being upset, being mad, sitting in a chair doing nothing, or playing the flute. If we stay stressed without soothing our self, we get more stressed. If we soothe our self so we feel relaxed; we become calmer, more focused and feel much more content and at peace.

The purpose of de-stressing is to become calm enough and available enough to access, develop and use all of the gifts and talents within you.

Be Aware

It is absolutely normal when we want to change, there is a part of us that wants to keep things just the way they are, even if they are uncomfortable and are not good for us. Some people call this the devil, the enemy, or the ego. However you think of this opposing force, be aware of it lurking to try to stop you from being your best self. If you know it is there, you can be prepared to deal with it. I'll give you some tools to deal with this negative voice later on.

When you have tools to soothe yourself, it is easy to stay calm and focused. Addictive behavior begins because we can't soothe our self. It makes perfect sense to want to eliminate stress, upsets, and unpleasant feelings. Without ways to soothe our self, we numb the body and mind with additive behaviors – drugs, alcohol, food, sex, compulsions such as keeping things in order, buying, cleaning, etc.

Here are two tools I use when I get scared. They are fast and easy to immediately de-stress when you feel scared, stuck, upset or frustrated:

1. Place an invisible shield all around you (like a thick glass bubble) so that only good can penetrate – all bad things bounce off it and back to the sender. I picture only good things entering the bubble.

2. Memorize and recite this Unity Prayer of Protection:

The light of God surrounds me
The love of God enfolds me
The power of God protects me
The presence of God watches over me
Wherever I am, God is

FOURTH TOOL: Mind Your Mind

Be a silent witness (like an observer on your shoulder who watches and hears everything you think, say, and do). This is a potent self-mastery tool that will bring you freedom. If you observe your thoughts, you are in a powerful position to change them on the spot. As an example, you might wake up and think, *another day in this hell hole.* With observation and your free choice, you can re-think and say, "Cancel that. I'm a healthy, strong person with unlimited ideas, thoughts, and ability – I choose to create something new and good today." You get to choose. The more you observe and choose to change your thoughts, the better life gets.

Freedom and power come first by observing yourself (without judgment) and deciding to keep or cancel what you just thought. I say *without judgment,* because it is very easy to bully ourselves when we catch our self thinking things we do not like. So, whenever you observe a thought or behavior, I suggest you use this comment: "Hummmmm, how interesting." Pretend you are a scientist gathering data to learn more about yourself. Scientists just gather facts, they don't judge and they don't say mean things about what they find. They simply watch and learn.

As you observe with a neutral attitude and an interest in discovering more about you, the more command you have over your life. And the best part is, the less power others have over you.

Wayne Dyer told this story as an example of growing awareness (or consciousness):

Day 1 - You walk down the street, you don't see a hole so you fall in it.

Day 2 - You walk down the street, you see a hole and you fall in it.

Day 3 - You walk down the street, you know a hole is there but you fall in it.

Day 4 - You walk down the street, you know a hole is there and you walk around it.

Day 5 - You walk down a different street.

Tell a Different Story

Have you noticed that you have a running dialogue in your mind and you keep telling yourself the same things over and over? When we keep telling the same story, the neuro-pathways in our brain become ruts just as dirt roads get worn into deep ruts by wagon or bicycle wheels. If you've ridden a bike on a dirt road, you know how difficult it is to get out of a rut.

Can you imagine if we said out loud what we say to ourselves? We might be called a bully, a vicious person or even a psycho.

Telling a different story means that we must wake up and listen to what we say to ourselves.

As mentioned before, at 17, when I awoke to my thoughts, I did not like what I was thinking and saying to myself. I was judgmental, arrogant, cynical, and spent nearly all my energy trying to look superior and keep myself safe. I was missing the joy of life.

Until that day, when a professor told us to pay attention to our thoughts and actions, I didn't know the story I was telling myself. I didn't know I had a whole script about me. It was only my narrow perspective based on my limited years of experience.

Because I was abused by my father and brother, and was unprotected by my mother, my old story was I was damaged and unlovable. I made up the rest of the story that said, unless I was always perfect, I would remain unlovable and unaccepted. Those thoughts drove me to be hyper-vigilant, constantly guarding myself against imagined danger, an over-achiever, and a compulsive manager of my life and those around me.

I ran away from home to escape and find a safer, happier world. What I found instead was myself.

I began to tell myself a different story. My new story was that I was courageous, strong and willing to do whatever it took to get through school. I was smart and did well. In time, I told myself that I was part of something bigger; that I was loved as a child of God and was guided and protected.

My story keeps changing as I appreciate my gifts and talents and as I find new ways to express and serve.

So what's your story? What are you telling yourself about your situation and your life? What are you saying about your community, your country, your world? What are you saying about your relationship, your past, your potential, your parents, and the people around you?

Are you thinking and speaking words of love, appreciation and acceptance? Or have you created a story in your mind that you are trying to make others fit into?

FIFTH TOOL: See Things Differently - Byron Katie's Questions

When my twin grandsons were very young, I drove them to school a few mornings a week. One boy usually kept me waiting. Although I said nothing, I told myself a story that he was lucky to be chauffeured to school in a comfortable car and I was doing him a favor taking my valuable time to drive him. Further, he didn't regard my time because he kept me waiting.

When I worked this issue through Byron Katie's questions, everything changed.

Set-up statement: This boy doesn't respect my time.

1. Can I know that this is true? No.

2. Can I really know that this is true? No.

3. How would I be without this thought? Free, free, free.

4. Turn-around thoughts: *I'm* not using my time wisely. I looked at all the ways that *I* don't respect myself. *I* distract myself with computer games; *I* watch too much TV, etc. It was not about him at all. This tool pointed to areas I needed to clean up in order to be a more productive, responsible person.

Here is another example of using Byron Katie's 4 questions.
Set-up statement: Tom doesn't understand me.

1. Can I know that this is true? No.

2. Can I really know that this is true? No.

3. How would I be without this thought? Free, free, free.

4. Turn-around thoughts: I don't understand Tom, I don't understand me.

SIXTH TOOL: Tapping

A most powerful tool I offer you is called Emotional Freedom Technique, or EFT tapping.

I had no idea I was claustrophobic until I needed to have an MRI done. This medical procedure consists of being rolled into a tiny tunnel of an MRI machine so pictures can be taken to determine what's going on inside the body. I had worked with clients who had panic attacks, so when I was rolled into the MRI machine, I recognized that I was having an attack. I felt like I was going to be crushed to death by the machine. My reaction startled me. I calmly said to the technician, "I must be claustrophobic so get me out of here." I told him that I would work on my fear and would reschedule another appointment when I felt able to do so.

In addition to feeling like a panic attack victim, I was blind-sided by the observation that I immediately began to scold myself for being unable to control my fear of being in close quarters.

I told two colleagues what happened and they both asked if I had tried EFT tapping. I knew the technique but never used it myself. After using this tapping tool, I was able to successfully have two necessary MRI's. I'm happy to report, I experienced them with (almost) ease and holding the hand of my daughter, Patricia.

Since then, I've attended two EFT World Summits and learned there are different techniques used in different parts of the world. I'll offer you a basic technique that I use and you can vary it, as you wish.

EFT tapping changes our thinking and feelings on a cellular level by tapping specific meridian pressure points in the body while speaking our problem out loud. Acupressure and acupuncture recognize the value of touching meridian pressure points. Dramatic change occurs when words are added to the tapping sequence because it not only shifts the cellular memory, but our neuro-pathways change as we say different phrases.

Reference the diagram while I tell you the points and the sequence, and then we'll practice together so you can get an idea how to do this.

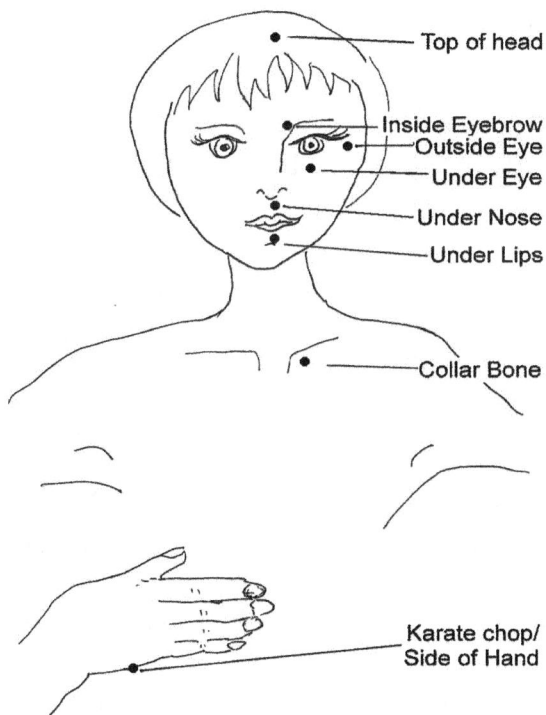

Top of head

Inside Eyebrow
Outside Eye
Under Eye
Under Nose
Under Lips

Collar Bone

Karate chop/
Side of Hand

Each point gets five to fifteen taps – firm enough to be felt but gentle enough so taps are not painful.

1. Start on the outside of the hand where you would give a karate chop.

2. Inside of the eyebrow, between one eyebrow toward the center forehead and just beyond the eyebrow hair.

3. Outside of eye on the bone where it curves in toward the eye.

4. Under the eye on the bone.

5. Under the nose.

6. Under the lips in the crease above the chin.

7. Collar bone –below your throat is a U-shaped bone that slopes outward – move 2-3" out along that bone.

8. Tap the inside of the wrists together OR top of head.

I use the tips of my index, middle and ring fingers to tap all areas except the collar bone, where I use an open hand.

As I begin with the Karate chop, I take some deep breaths and I establish on an intensity scale of 1-10 (ten being the most severe) how strong the emotion is. For example, I'm going to go back in time when I had a panic attack in the MRI machine and my intensity number was 10 on my scale.

Just as I use my claustrophobia as an example, you pick a situation where you feel blocked or fearful and substitute your own words or situation. It might be "I can't get along with my boss, I'm fearful I'll fail my test, I'm scared I won't have enough money, I can't stand this pain. I can't handle this stress." Whatever your situation is, identify it now and we'll call it "the set-up statement." Take a deep breath and give it a number (0 to 10) on the intensity scale.

Here we go with the set-up statement: "Even though I'm claustrophobic, (fill in your own set-up statement), I deeply and completely accept myself."

1. Karate chop place on the side of the hand: "Even though I'm claustrophobic, I deeply and completely accept myself."

2. Inside of the eyebrow tap 10 times. "Even though I'm claustrophobic, I deeply and completely accept myself."

3. Outside of eye: "Even though I'm claustrophobic, I deeply and completely accept myself."

4. Under eye, tap 10 times: "Even though I'm claustrophobic, I deeply and completely accept myself."

5. Tap under nose: "Even though I'm claustrophobic, I deeply and completely accept myself."

6. Tap under lips: "Even though I'm claustrophobic, I deeply and completely accept myself."

7. Pat with open hand over your collar bone: "Even though I'm claustrophobic, I deeply and completely accept myself."

8. Tap the inside of your wrists together: "Even though I'm claustrophobic, I deeply and completely accept myself."

Take a deep breath and evaluate 1-10 how you are feeling after round one. I suggest you tap until your level of intensity is three or below.

Please note that the intensity *may* increase rather than decrease at first. This is a good thing because you are allowing deeper feelings to arise. Keep tapping and see what happens. It will delight you.

This process shifts the emotional response in the body. The tapping tool is effective to get you through traumatic situations.

For total healing, you can heal more deeply by adding an additional process. Here is an example:

As you tap through each pressure point, your additional statements might change to:

"Every cell, organ and tissue in my body is free."

"Every fiber, bone, muscle and tendon in my body is free."

"I am whole and complete."

SEVENTH TOOL: Communication

When we talk with someone we are either saying, "I love you" or "Help me."

Compassionate Communication, as taught by Dr. Michael Rosenberg, is a valuable skill because it helps us get what we want.

The giraffe is the land mammal with the largest heart (because it needs to pump blood all the way up the long neck to the brain.) So listening like a Giraffe means to listen from your heart so you hear beneath the words.

When someone sounds upset, they are really saying, "Help me." Having compassion allows us to respond to someone's unspoken need.

For example, if your partner comes home tired and upset and grumbles, "I'm hungry! When's dinner?" He/she is saying, "Help me get rid of these hunger pangs and feed me so I feel soothed."

Instead of getting angry and starting a fight, hear "help me" underneath the words. Offer a quick snack to take the edge off hunger if a meal isn't ready. You'll be delighted to see how quickly a relationship can move to a deeper connection when we listen for "help me" beneath the words.

As valuable as it is to listen to others with a big heart, it is most important to help yourself. Each hour of the day and night, ask yourself, "How do I feel? What do I need?" These questions will keep you in balance and in control of your own life.

Compassionate communication gets us what we want and helps others feel safe and at ease around us.

We've all known people who act as if their only tool was a hammer – they beat up people when they get frustrated. They have no other tools to use. How much easier and joyful life would be if we all had useful tools.

I once worked for a company who manufactured medical devices. Our tiny administrative office was attached to a warehouse. We received shipments of raw material and components by truck that would then be stored then shipped to our manufacturing plant. Our company policy was that *only* the warehouse manager or general manager were permitted to accept deliveries.

One day, both the warehouse and general manager were gone. A trucker arrived with a shipment. The receptionist told him we could not accept his shipment and he would have to come back or wait for a manager. He began yelling and swearing. She was so afraid that she ran to get me, hoping I could calm him down. I told him he had every right to be upset because we messed up his schedule. I told him I'd be upset too. He calmed down immediately when he knew I was on his side. I suggested he take a short lunch break and try a fabulous taco shop down the street then come back.

He did this and when he returned, he said the food was great and thanked me for the suggestion. The general manager was back, we received his delivery and he was on his way. That is an example of compassionate communication – understanding what the other person must be feeling and responding in a way that reflects we understand. Powerful relationships occur when we place ourselves in the other person's shoes to feel what they might be experiencing and respond in a kind, caring way.

EIGHTH TOOL: Ask for Help
(use resources around you)

I was raised to believe it wasn't okay to ask for help. Were you? If so, then it is time to change that thought. Not only is it *okay* to ask for help; we are all here to help one another. I've noticed that the more we ask, the farther we go. Interestingly, the more we help others, the more successful we become.

One way to ask for help is to write or call a friend. Ask if she or he is willing to let you talk out a problem without giving you advice. As you hear yourself talk, you may hear the solution you are seeking. If your friend is wise, you may want to ask for feedback or advice.

If you still need help, contact someone who has overcome your problem, situation, or challenge. Find someone who has solved your same issue. People want to help you plus you are giving them an opportunity to share their experience and successes with you.

Another way to ask for help is to use your library. It is a gold mine *filled* with treasures. Ask the librarians and assistants for help. They are masters at navigating you to resources that uncover your answers. They are wise and wonderful people, so use them. They want to help you.

Answers to

Life's Toughest Questions

Abundance

Why do I struggle so much and have so little?

Struggle may be what you are used to seeing and experiencing. If your belief is "Life is tough and then you die," chances are, that is what you'll experience.

Wealth is a state of mind. You can think poor or you can think rich. If you have health, love, food, and a place to sleep, and inner freedom, you are rich.

You may not have what you want, but you have what you need. If you want to increase your abundance, start by being grateful, and blessing everything you have.

Declare: My heart is open to receive God's good. I'm grateful for what I have, and I freely share with others.

Acceptance

Why don't people like me?

Chances are, you are the one who doesn't like you. Change your story about yourself. Start a story about your wonderful qualities, and how lovable and special you are.

Love yourself as you are, yet develop qualities that you appreciate in others. Would you choose yourself as a best friend?

Like yourself and everyone else.

Declare: I like me, I like others, and they like me.

Accidents

Why do accidents always happen to me?

If you are counting all your mishaps, you are gathering evidence to prove you are a victim. Is it possible you are focusing on what's wrong instead of what's right?

Accidents are incidents that happen to everyone. How you deal with unexpected circumstances shows the quantity and quality of your coping tools.

Instead of crying in stormy weather, learn to dance in the rain.

Declare: I make the best of every situation because it is all good.

Addiction

Why do I have an addiction?

Have compassion for yourself. You just want to soothe yourself to stop the pain. When the pain returns, you soothe yourself again and again. If you have not been able to end the cycle of addiction, get help. 12-step programs and treatment centers are available to you and they can work if you make the effort to make them work for you.

Instead of hating yourself because you just want to feel better, get help today. Your life can turn around the moment you decide to turn it around.

Declare: There is help for me, and I choose to get it now.

Adjustment

Why am I always the one that has to adjust?

People who will not budge are too frightened to move. They fear change.

If you are willing to give up something for a higher purpose (to get the job done, to move forward, etc.), that shows you are indeed the stronger person.

Stand for who you are and what you believe, but be willing to bend when needed.

Declare: I am strong enough to bend, and I will not break.

Age

Why am I feeling like I want to look younger?

Aging means we are moving toward death. Some people fear death. In the Western culture, great value is placed on youth and beauty. We obsess about looking young and looking good.

Eastern culture reveres the elderly. Asians have healthier bodies and live longer lives and don't seem to fret about youth or beauty.

Declare: I am timeless and ageless and am exactly where I am supposed to be.

Agreements

I don't cheat people so why am I being sued?

If everyone did what was right, there would be no need for lawyers or the judicial system.

Greedy people are afraid they won't have enough so they fear they will be cheated. They strike out to grab and feel powerful, even if hurts another. Power makes them feel safe.

Declare: I live my life doing what I know is right. I make agreements up front so everyone knows what is expected. My power comes from knowing I am doing the right thing.

Anger

Why do I get so angry?

Emotions dwell within, and no one can make you angry. Being angry is a decision you make.

If you have not learned to use words to express yourself calmly, you are more likely to exhibit outbursts of anger. It has nothing to do with another person or circumstance.

Declare: I can express my feelings calmly.

Answers

Why do people expect me to have all the answers?

The more information you have, the more guidance and wisdom you can share with others. It is natural for others to gravitate to a point of information when they need guidance.

While having lots of information is useful, however, being curious opens doors to exploration. Discovering new things keeps you vibrant and fascinating to others.

Declare: I am open to learn and I help others. I can show them where to find information.

Anxiety

Why do I worry so much?

The human brain loves to figure out puzzles. It naturally creates problems to solve and loves to ponder things.

Worrying gives you practice handling the emotions you might feel when you are faced with change. Worrying can be your way to practice problem-solving. I've heard this called future-organizing.

The down-side of playing what-if games is that it keeps you from being present in the moment, which is the *only* place change can happen.

Declare: In the now, there is no worry.

Balance

Why do I feel out of balance most of the time?

You can only re-balance by noticing when you are out of balance.

Unless you feel over-tired, you don't get the message to rest. When you feel restless, you get the urge to exercise.

To stay in balance, ask yourself throughout the day, "How do I feel? What do I need?"

Declare: I bring myself into balance by listening to my needs and responding.

Beauty

Why do I feel ugly?

Beauty is perception plus attitude. Aside from the geometric balance of facial features, beauty is exhibited in the way you carry yourself plus what you think of yourself on the inside.

People who radiate love, kindness and confidence shine with beauty. People who are blessed with beautiful features become ugly by their negative, unkind natures.

Beauty is as beauty does. Nothing is more beautiful than a loving, compassionate, kind heart.

Declare: My love shines so brightly that it colors the world beautiful.

Being Me

Why can't I just be myself?

Civil codes of conduct require you follow rules in public. We wear clothes, behave respectfully to people, animals and property, etc.

At home alone, you can always be yourself and you need to express yourself, be creative, share your gifts, experience all of life, do what you love, say what you feel, share your dreams, and have hope for the future. Do it in a considerate, respectful way and others will appreciate you and your individuality.

Declare: I'm free to be me.

Blame

Why do I get blamed for things?

Blame is holding someone else responsible for an out-come.

Generally there are two stories – in one story, you say someone else is to blame, so you are innocent. In the other story you tell yourself that you are the victim and get blamed without cause. In both stores, you take no responsibility.

Here's the deal – when you point your finger at someone else, notice you have 3 of your fingers pointing back at you. When you take responsibility for your actions and make corrections, you will no longer be blamed.

Declare: I take full responsibility for situations in my life. I get through them and move on.

Building Bridges

What does it mean to build bridges?

Bridges span obstacles (such as water) to get you where you want to go.

Relationships can be like bridges when one person connects you with someone who can get you where you are going faster and more easily. Also, you may be the bridge that connects people.

A huge benefit of being kind and considerate to everyone is that you never know when someone will come back into your life to support you.

Declare: Everyone I meet is worthy of respect and kindness.

Burdens/Stress

Stress – Why is my life so hard?

Compared to what? If you are feeling life is hard, you need tools to make it easier. A burden or stress points you toward finding a new tool to ease your burden.

Stress is worrying about something that has not happened yet or re-telling yourself a story of something that has already happened.

It is hard work to try to manage issues that have past or have not happened yet. No wonder life seems hard.

Get back into the present moment and ask yourself, "What can I release? What can I put to rest? What must be done in this exact moment?"

Declare: I only have power in this moment. I stay present to use this power.

Business

What does it mean when people say, "This is just business?"

We all have feelings. When someone's mind disagrees with his heart, he says, "This is just business." It is a way to follow the rules without feeling the pain of doing something that hurts another.

Doing what is right means being fair and considerate so everyone wins.

Declare: I do all my business fairly and with kindness.

Caring for Others

Why do I feel like I have to take care of everybody?

You take care of your children because it is your responsibility; you take care of your frail parents because it is the right thing to do. We are here to help others. If the burden is too heavy, you have taken on more than it your share.

Taking care of others can also cripple them if they are not given opportunities to learn, struggle, make mistakes and blossom. You decide if you are caring for or crippling another.

Declare: I do what I can to make the lives of others easier, when they are unable to make their own lives easier.

Cheerfulness

Why put on a happy face?

Why not? Cheerfulness is your natural state. Babies and toddlers have cheery dispositions and practice instant forgiveness. They look forward to learning and trying new things.

Emotions which last more than 10 minutes have nothing to do with the present circumstance. If you are feeling sad or mad longer than 10 minutes, you are pulling emotions from the past. Feel what you feel, then get over it.

Declare: My pleasant attitude makes a difference in the world.

Children

Am I supposed to like kids?

You are free to like or not like any individuals or groups. Ask yourself the following:

1. Exactly what makes me uncomfortable, annoyed, or afraid around kids?

2. What good or bad experiences have I had?

3. Do I know what, if anything is expected of me around kids?

4. How different am I from the person who does like kids?

Declare: I'm free to enjoy my likes and I appreciate others who have different likes.

Claiming My Place

Why don't I fit in?

Humans are created as individualized, personalized, one-of-a-kind models. You are not a carbon copy of anyone else, yet we long to belong.

Being with those who share common activities gives people a sense of oneness. Do you see the things that you have in common with others, or do you dwell on the differences? Find those activities that you can enjoy with others, and you will be where you fit in.

Declare: I am a unique combination of special talents. I enjoy being with others who share some of these.

Cleanliness

Is cleanliness really next to Godliness?

Two of the 12 aspects of God are described as balance and order. When we and our things are in balance and in order, cleanliness is present.

Declare: I keep myself clean and my things clean and orderly.

Confidence

How can I stop being shy?

Shyness is an excuse to avoid the scary stuff like showing up, speaking up, and living life.

Confidence comes from being shy or scared and doing it anyway. Every time we walk through a fear, we build confidence.

Declare: I choose to walk through fear because confidence awaits me on the other side.

Confusion

Why can't I make a decision?

If you are fearful of making a wrong decision, allow yourself to change your mind. Few decisions are life-threatening. In other words, allow yourself to re-choose if your first choice didn't work out.

When there is a pull between your intuition and the information you have gathered, you will be confused.

If you don't know the consequences for each option, find out.

Declare: Every decision I make is perfect for the moment. I can always re-choose.

Courage

Why am I scared?

Fear is hard-wired into us from caveman days to keep us safe. Without fear, we would be extinct. However, we live in a safe world with lots of tools.

If you have taken sensible steps to protect yourself and your property, your fear may be a story you are telling yourself.

Although you can't control what other people think or do, you can control what you think. Don't scaring yourself. Use your strength and energy to live a wonderful life.

Declare: Whatever happens, I'll be able to handle it.

Crisis Thinking

What is crisis thinking?

Knowing there is a solution to every problem, and finding that solution quickly is crisis thinking.

Because stress, fear and panic cause foggy thinking during emergencies, you need emergency plans set up in advance.

Call a friend who will be the voice of reason when you need one.

Declare: My family has a plan of action in an emergency, and we all know what to do.

Criticism

Why can't I stop criticizing others?

During early childhood the brain develops the keen ability to find flaws. Practice makes perfect. If you grew up with someone who criticized, you probably learned to criticize.

Find a positive way to use this ability! Quality Control, Design and Editing are three fields where your talents are needed. Make things better – offer the changes you desire to see.

Declare: If there is a better way, I'll find it.

Death

Is everyone afraid of death?

People who fear death generally are in these categories:

1. I might feel pain.

2. I'll be alone forever.

3. My loved ones will feel pain.

4. I haven't yet lived my dreams.

When we experience a loss, every previous loss comes to mind so we re-live that grief on top of the current loss.

Is it possible that death is a threshold to another dimension in which our Spirit lives on forever?

Declare: I live every moment with vigor and vitality so I have no regrets.

Debt

Will I ever get out of debt?

You get into debt by buying stuff to soothe emptiness. What are you really, really seeking?

People get into debt for three reasons:

1. They don't distinguish between a want and a need.

2. They do not live within their means.

3. They don't ask for help when needed.

Declare: I pay cash for what I need. If I want something, I save until I can pay cash for it.

Depression

Is everybody depressed?

The World Health Organization names depression as the second largest cause of disability so you know you aren't alone.

To climb out of your depression, find a safe place to feel the anger toward others or yourself that you have pushed down.

Do not send it, but write a letter to the people you feel caused you pain, describing in detail how you feel. Then read it aloud, feel it, then burn it. Pound pillows, if it helps.

Declare: I will express my feelings in the right time and place so I am free.

Different People

Why do I get creeped out when I see crippled people?

Anything unusual or different may create an inner conflict of emotions. Perhaps you are curious yet unfamiliar and don't want to embarrass another.

Is it possible that different people are lights who come to earth to remind us to appreciate every blessing we have and to look beyond appearances to find the treasures and possibilities that dwell within ourselves and others?

Declare: I love and bless all people.

Economic Security

Why don't I feel safe?

It is not about money; it is knowing you will be cared for no matter what.

You have been cared for up to now – you are here and you are alive. Trust that you will be okay regardless of how much or little money you have.

Declare: I am always provided for.

Employment

Why can't I find a job that makes me happy?

Figure out what your talents and gifts are. Read Barbara Sher's book Live *the Life You Love.*

Figure out what your values are. Read my book, *Get Unstuck Live with Ease*. Read the Values page and do the exercise.

Then match your gifts, talents, and values to a job. You will love going to work and getting paid doing what is easy and fun.

Declare: I use my gifts and live my values so work is joyful.

Enlightenment

Are some people really enlightened?

Be wary of anyone who tells you he or she is enlightened.

Enlightenment comes from practicing the presence of God. Be still and go within. Illumination, understanding, and clarification are there for you.

Trust your own judgment. Discern when someone is sincere.

Declare: In the silence, I am one with enlightenment.

Enthusiasm

What's so great about being enthusiastic?

No one is forcing you to be dialed in, turned on, and plugged into the game of life. You can be a spectator and watch.

Enthusiasm shows you are connected to life's passion and are truly alive. Discover what you are passionate about and go for it.

Declare: Life is to be lived so count me in on the game.

Envy

Why do so many people have better stuff than I do?

When you compare, you will never be satisfied because there is always someone who has better stuff. Do you place value on material things and equate stuff with success or achievement?

Stuff is just stuff and has nothing to do with your personal value.

Inventory your talents and virtues and value who you are. Be grateful for your uniqueness because you are one-of-a-kind model.

Declare: I value who I am and what I do.

Exercise

I hate to exercise but feel guilty when I don't. Why is this?

Our bodies call for exercise to be balanced and healthy. There are activities that you may not consider to be exercise, such as dancing, walking, skating, swimming, snowboarding, surfing, or gardening that you may enjoy.

Find an exercise that you love and it won't feel like work. What is fun to you? If you are serious about a regular exercise program, ask a friend to join you and keep you accountable for showing up regularly.

Declare: It feels wonderful to use my muscles and move my body.

Expectation

Why don't I get what I want?

1. Your expectations are unrealistic – don't expect your cat to iron your shirt.

2. You weren't crystal clear about what you wanted.

3. You didn't make your wishes known.

4. You haven't done the work needed – you can't be a pilot without flight lessons and a license.

Declare: I know what I want, I do what is needed, and I'll roll with the punches if things don't turn out as I expected.

Eyes

Why don't I see what other people see?

Seeing things differently may be a great gift. How are you using this gift? Visual perception is not right or wrong, just different.

Perception is your view filtered by your story. If your story is, "I'm not ok," you tint everything you see and experience to prove your theory that you are not ok. If your perception is everything I see will make my life more wonderful, that is what you will see and experience.

Declare: I clearly see what is before me without filters.

Faith

Can a person get faith or do you have to always have it?

Everyone has faith. You have faith that your chair will hold you when you sit down; that your food will not poison you . . . you just don't think about it.

Faith is knowing that no matter what, you are going to be okay. You can strengthen faith (like muscles), by using them. The more faith you use, the more faith you have.

Declare: All is well. All is well.

Family

Why did I get stuck with a crazy family?

Is it possible that you were born into the only family that could mold you into the person you were meant to be?

Is it possible that what you wanted most from your family is what you are meant to give to yourself and to others?

There are absolute gifts in all situations. Find the gifts and you'll find joy and peace of mind.

Declare: My family is just right for me and I am just right for them.

Fatigue

Why do I feel so tired all the time?

Three emotional things drain us:

You resist what you are doing. If you love what you do, time flies and you stay energized.

You don't listen to your body. Stop and refresh yourself.

You have unfinished mental tasks. Returning a call, telling someone "no," making an appointment, washing the car - we are energized when we finish our mental "to do" lists.

Declare: I enjoy what I am doing, I rest when I am tired, and I my mental to-do list is up to date.

Food

Why can't I eat normally? I over eat or think about food all the time.

A relationship with food is not about having a party in your mouth, you are numbing your senses.

Food is fuel for the body – nothing more. Ask yourself, what does my body need?

Stop asking what you want; start asking what you need.

Declare: I eat what I need when I need it, and stop when I have it.

Forgiving

Why can't I forgive others?

People hold onto anger because they think it gives them strength to avoid pain in the future.

Forgiving another isn't for them, it is for you. You imprison yourself and stay glued to an upset until you forgive yourself and others. It isn't about being right or wrong, it is about seeing they or you did their best at the time (as you did.) Forgive them and yourself and move on. Then you become free.

Declare: I am strong enough to handle whatever happens.

Freedom

Will I ever be free? I can't see the light at the end of the tunnel.

The hole you're in might be deep, dark, and long, but if you look up, you will see the light. You dug the hole. The same strength you used to dig the hole is available to dig yourself out.

Ask for help. What do you need? Who can help? What resources are available? God is with you.

Declare: Freedom is a choice. Each prisoner can choose to look skyward or into the mud. Look up.

Friends

I don't have a lot of friends. What's wrong with me?

Quantity is not better than quality. One or two great friends are better than three dozen acquaintances.

Are you a good friend to others? Do you show up and stand with someone in need? Do you take turns listening? Focus more on being a friend and you will get more friends.

Declare: I am a great friend and I can be counted on when needed.

Frustration

How do I avoid going off the deep end?

Pay attention to how you feel. Your feelings serve as a compass because they tell you if you are going in a good direction.

When you get irritated, agitated, or upset, pay attention and clear things up as they come along. Don't wait and implode on yourself or explode on others.

Use your new tools to deal with stress.

Declare: I handle upsets as they come along.

Gardening

Gardening is boring. It takes too long and I hate getting dirty. Is that wrong?

It isn't wrong to have preference. When you call something boring, are you describing yourself?

Gardening is a metaphor for life – there are seasons and cycles, and if we work with the seasons, we will reap a rich harvest. We clear the plot, prepare the soil, plant the seeds, water, weed, wait patiently, harvest, and appreciate what we've grown. Then we begin again.

Declare: My garden produces rich vegetables and flowers to enjoy and to bless others.

Getting Along

Why is it so hard to get along with others?

Since you are the common denominator in all relationships, pay attention to what happens at the moment you don't get along. Are you attached to being right? Are you listening quietly? Do you respect the ideas of others? Do you have a picture of how others should be?

Playing well with others is a learned skill. Watch skillful people interact then learn effective tools they use. Use compassionate communication and you will always get along.

Declare: I play well with others and respect them.

Gifts

How do I know what my gifts are?

Read Barbara Sher's book, *Live the Life you Love,* to find your inherent gifts.

What do you love to do? What would you do for no pay? What engages your heart and soul so time flies by? Those are your gifts.

Declare: My gifts guide me and always point to joy.

Gratitude

What is so important about being grateful?

A sincere sense of gratitude opens up floodgates for good to come to you. Having a grateful heart, is the first law of attraction. If you want more, be grateful for what you have.

Isn't it more fun to give to someone who is grateful than someone who scoffs at your gift?

Declare: I love what I have and what I get – it is all good.

Grief

What do you do when someone dies?

Show up and be with those who are grieving. You don't need to say anything and you don't even need to do anything. Be there.

Be willing to sit with them as they grieve. Stay with them until they feel strong enough to stay by themselves.

Declare: I will ease someone's pain by being present for them.

Guidance

How do I know what to do?

Be still and go within. You will have all the answers you need. Listen, trust what you hear. Be willing to do what you hear. Your greatest ally is trusting yourself.

Declare: I listen and heed the still, small whispers within.

Healing

Why are some people continually sick?

The body's natural state is one of balance and wellness. When one is sick, they are out of balance. Causes are poor nutrition, poor exercise or rest habits, stress, harmful addictions, and most of all, negative thinking. What we think about is what we become.

There is a payoff for being sick. Sick people may get more attention. They don't have to show up and be responsible. They get other people do things for them. They get to control their life around their illness.

Declare: I am radiantly healthy and balanced.

Heartache

Does everybody have heartache?

Sorrow, sadness, and despair come to all. What we do with it is important.

Whatever is here, it will pass. If you are going through hell, keep moving. Don't stop and live there.

Declare: I allow myself to feel misery, but I let it go so I feel joy again.

Home

I feel awful because I don't have a home. Is that bad?

Everyone has a home because we ARE our own home. Just as a tortoise carries his home on his back, we carry everything we need within us.

Home is a word, not always a physical place. Being at ease, being comfortable in your own skin, trusting your friends and your environment is being at home.

We can create a home for our self and others just by our consciousness. We can make others feel at home in our presence.

A place to call home gives us peace. Trust your place is waiting for you and you will be there soon.

Declare: I welcome all and all welcome me.

Ideas

Why can't I think of great ideas?

What makes you think you don't think of great things? Perhaps you are sharing your ideas with the wrong people. Share your ideas with people who value and appreciate you and what you have to offer. If you change your friends, you'll find out what wonderful ideas you have.

You are as smart as you need to be.

Declare: I have great ideas that are of value to me and others.

Jail

How can being in jail be beneficial?

Being locked up stops life so you have an opportunity to slow down and look at how your life is going. You can evaluate what changes you want to make. It gives you an opportunity to turn your life around. Jail can be a perfect time to make major life changes. It gives you time to learn new tools, ponder, to meditate, to pray, to write, to re-choose ways of being in the world.

Declare: I use this time to change my thinking and change my life.

Jealousy

Why am I jealous?

Because you are afraid you are not enough to keep someone. Trust that you are enough.

If someone leaves you, you are better off without them. Why keep someone who wants to be somewhere else?

What you fear the most, you bring to you so just be your best, authentic self and trust your perfect partner will be attracted to you and will want to stay.

Declare: I will love you while you are here. If you leave, I'll be fine.

Journaling

What's the big deal about keeping a journal?

Journaling moves thoughts, fears and emotions from the inside to the outside where there is more light. In other words, you can see things more clearly when they are on paper.

Be sure to keep your writing in a safe place – it is only for your eyes.

Declare: I write to free inner thoughts, fears, dreams, and emotions.

Kindness

Why should I be kind? People aren't kind to me.

If you want to be treated with kindness, treat others kindly.

It is our nature to be kind, to respect others and to share freely.
Any other behavior stems from past pain, fear and your thoughts
about yourself.

Declare: I am kind and others are kind in return.

Listening to Your Inner Voice

How Can I trust the voices within?

If the inner voice sounds loving, kind, gentle and there is no rush, it is God.

If the voice prompts you to care for yourself – brush your teeth; if it wants the BEST for you, to keep you safe, it is God. It holds you in the light and knows you are capable.

If the voice has urgency, is loud, bossy, filled with fear, it is not God but EGO (Edging God Out.) It is against you. Some call it the devil. If it taunts you, tempts you or bullies you; if it is never satisfied and reminds you of all the negatives, it is NOT God.

Declare: Only the voice of God shall be heard from within. All other voices have no merit.

Listening

What if I hate to listen?

Perhaps you are with people to talk too much. If you haven't given yourself a voice, then it makes sense that listening would be difficult.

Speak up, speak out and others will listen to you.

Declare: I have something to say that is worthy of being heard.

Loneliness

Why do I feel lonely?

Loneliness comes from being disconnected from your own soul. Spend time in silence, get to know yourself, become friends with yourself and you will never be lonely again.

Be there for others and you will feel less lonely.

Declare: I am connected and at home with myself. I'm never alone.

Loss

How can losing someone be beneficial?

As painful as loss might be, it can lead us inward where comfort and unity dwells. It can make space for someone more wonderful to enter your life.

Declare: I am sad to lose someone dear, and am certain someone wonderful is waiting to walk into my life.

Love

Will I ever find true love?

You ARE true love. Begin by honoring, appreciating and cherishing yourself.

BE the love you are seeking. In other words, become what you are looking for. Your partner is looking for you.

Declare: I am love, I am loving, and I am loved.

Magic

Is there such a thing as magic?

A miracle is another word for magic. I believe in miracles because I see them all around me. A mighty oak rising up from a tiny acorn is magic. A colorful rainbow after a storm is magical. Finding lost objects, thinking of someone and they call you is magic, and lighting up a child's face is pure magic.

Declare: I believe in magic – it makes life more exciting, mysterious and joyful.

Manipulation

Do most people manipulate?

Everyone wants to have things go their way. Pay attention to your intentions. Notice when you manipulate the situation. If you are clear and up front with yourself, and you are absolutely certain no one is hurt in any way, manipulation is fine.

Declare: I am aware of my intention. I hurt no one intentionally.

Marriage

Is it better to be married?

Yes for some and no for others. Trust your intuition. If you feel it is right and your emotions are joyful and peaceful, then it is right for you. If you feel it is something you ought to do but you are hesitant and not sure this is the right time or the right person, you are probably right.

Declare: Marriage is a personal choice and I'll know when and if marriage is right for me.

Mentoring

Does everyone need a mentor?

We have mentors whether we know it or not. We notice how people live and we emulate them.

People watch us and want to be like us.

Life is easier when we have a hand to hold and someone who will help us reach our goals. Life Coaches can be perfect mentors.

Declare: I live in a way that my life is worthy of mentoring another.

Mothers and Fathers

Why does it matter to me what my mother or father thinks?

A mother and father stand for unconditional love – they loved us even when we had dirty diapers.

We get esteem from their love and want to please them so they will continue loving us.

What is most important is what *you* think of you. Tell yourself what you wanted to hear from your mother and father.

Declare: I am the best parent to myself because I say what I wanted to hear.

My Place

Why don't I feel I belong?

When we don't feel we fit in, we have told our self a story that
we are so different from others that we have no place here. A
more powerful story to tell yourself is that you are more like
others than you are different. Find similarities: You are human,
you breathe, your DNA is very similar, you have feelings,
concerns, and families, etc.

When we find commonalities, we feel a closer fit with others.
Our thoughts determine whether we fit or don't fit - nothing
more.

Declare: I have a right to be here. I belong.

Nature

Why do I want to be outdoors most of the time?

Nature is healing, calming, balancing and re-generating. It makes sense you would want to be outdoors.

If you must be indoors, bring as much nature into your space as possible – plants, fresh flowers, small trees, natural fabrics, branches, wood, a water fountain, etc. Honor your need to connect with nature.

Declare: I am part of nature and it is a part of me.

Nutrition

How do I know who to believe about the best diet?

Gather general information then start writing down what you eat and how you feel. You will learn that certain foods and drinks work really well for your body and others don't.

When you listen, your body will guide you to what you need for optimum health.

Read: *Forks over Knives* by Gene Stone and *The Evolutionary Diet by* Dr. Gundry.

Declare: I eat what I need and feel wonderful.

Opinions

Why are people so opinionated?

An opinion is an attitude, judgment, view, or belief that we see through our own colored lenses.

While keeping one's opinion to oneself may be wise, we get to know others when we share preferences. We find similarities and new ways to connect.

Declare: I reserve judgments and share my preferences when asked.

Pain

Why have I had so much pain in my life?

Everyone experiences pain, loss, sadness, and upsets. Some experience more pain than others. A sobering phrase: "I cried because I had no shoes until I met a man who had no feet."

Painful experiences are turning points that lead to greater joy. Find a gift from a painful experience and you will find joy. As an example, if hardship taught you to new coping skills, that is a gift.

Focus on what is good and right and enriching and you will see more good come to you.

Declare: Life is happy, easy and joyful.

Partnerships

Why do my partnerships end up in divorce?

These are the key reasons partnerships don't last:

1. You haven't fully developed to be ready for marriage – cleaned up your baggage so you are fully mature.

2. You may not be well suited.

3. You haven't learned how to communicate.

4. You haven't created a plan for success.

5. You haven't learned to negotiate.

6. You haven't had good role models.

Before you walk down the aisle, accomplish the above, then:

1. Write a detailed list of what makes you feel happy, safe and secure.

2. Write another detailed list of deal-breakers; what behavior will cause you to pack your bag and leave?

If couples know what makes each other feel safe and what will cause them to bolt, everything in between is negotiable.

Declare: I'm blessed that my partner enriches my life.

Patience

What's so great about being patient?

Patience is the first sign of maturity. It shows we have mastered impulse control. We can wait, sit with discomfort, and we can gather facts before we respond.

Without patience, we react without thinking and that causes trouble.

Declare: I am patient and respond when the time is right.

Peace of Mind

Why is everybody looking for peace of mind?

Peace of mind comes from a spiritual communion. We are "home." We yearn to be close to God, where we feel safe and at home.

From an earthly perspective, we live in a hectic world that which produces anxiety, stress and even low-level panic.

Peace of mind is composure, serenity and calmness. We need balance and relief from stress. Peace of mind keeps us sane.

Declare: I am calm and serene, no matter what.

Pets

Is it wrong to love my pet so much?

Pets provide healing, comfort, companionship, and joy. Of course we would want to love our pets.

If you only love your pets and have no social interaction with humans, then it is time to build human friendships as well.

Declare: My pets add great joy to my life.

Play Dates

Do grown-ups need play dates?

We call them social engagements. However going on a play date by yourself can be valuable.

I highly recommend a daily walk outdoors as a play date. Fill up with nature's abundance of trees, shrubs, flowers, animals, and the sky.

Declare: I enjoy walking in nature and connecting with the beauty around me.

Power

Is it true that power make the world crazy?

The desire for power creates greed and wars. That sounds crazy to me.

Self-mastery means minding your own business, owning your own power, being responsible, and giving your gifts so you make a positive contribution to the planet.

Declare: I stand in my own power.

Prayer

Is it necessary to pray?

Science has proven that prayer changes the energy of matter so we know it works.

Prayer also changes the one praying. We shift into a posture of receptivity and prayer forces us to be clear about what we want when we ask in prayer.

Every thought is a prayer so stay tuned in to your thoughts to be sure you are inviting what you really, really want.

Declare: I pray for myself, for others, and for the planet.

Priorities

Why can't I figure out what do first?

You haven't learned how to establish priorities.

Ask yourself these questions:

1. What must absolutely get done in the next 5 minutes?

2. What must absolutely get done today, no matter what?

3. What must be done in the next day?

4. What may be done anytime this week?

Make a list and follow it.

Declare: I know what and when things need to be done.

Privacy

Is it wrong to be a private person?

Can you distinguish between privacy and secrecy?

Being private means you identify personal and financial information you wish to keep to yourself.

Being secretive is not revealing information because you fear the shame you will feel if others know your secret. Keeping family secrets, for instance, may isolate you from being in loving relationships.

Declare: I choose to keep some information private, but I'm free to be me.

Protection

Why do I feel scared most of the time?

No one taught you ways to feel safe. Memorize the Unity Prayer of Protections:

> *The light of God surrounds me.*
> *The love of God enfolds me.*
> *The power of God protects me.*
> *The presence of God watches over me.*
> *Wherever I am, God is.*

Memorize this chant:

> *God before me, God behind me, to the left and right.*
> *God above, God below me, all around and inside.*

Declare: I am always protected. I am safe.

Relaxation

What is the best way to relax?

Use the breathing techniques in this book. Consider using candles, listen to soothing music and getting still and going within.

Declare: I am relaxed and refreshed.

Release of Others

Why do I hang on even to people who are no good for me?

No one wants to face the pain of separation and loss. But this pain is better than staying in a hurtful, unhappy relationship.

You deserve better.

"But I love him" is a poor excuse to stay in a miserable situation. Let the person go so you will be free to receive a better partner.

Declare: I let go of everyone and everything that keeps me from my good.

Religion

Is it okay to have a different religion from my family or not even go to church?

Finding a religion, a path, or way of life that offers you the richest and greatest happiness is always right for you.

Whether you choose to follow a doctrine or not is also fine.

Your emotions will guide you. If you feel that going to church is unsatisfying or constricting, change churches or find another path. Your answers are within you. Listen and trust them.

Declare: I have a path that feels good and right. It fills me with deep satisfaction.

Resentment

Why can't I stop feeling upset over what happened to me?

You are telling yourself the same story over and over. Change your story. Tell yourself the good that you got from the situation and what you learned from it. Tell yourself that you got through it. Decide what you want in your future.

New story = new experiences.

Declare: I can change the story I tell myself. New stories bring freedom.

Responsibility

Why do people tell me to take responsibility?

When someone tells you what you already know inside, you don't like it because you have not listened to your own inner voice.

If people are telling you to take responsibility, ask yourself, "In what areas might I be more responsible?"

This is an opportunity to grow in a new way that will make your life happier.

Declare: I am responsible and it feels great to control my own life.

Risk-Taking

I'm afraid of change – why is that?

1. The unknown is scary because you haven't done it before. Clinging to what you know seems safer. With every new skill you have ever learned, you took a risk and you did it. You gave up crawling to walk.

2. Risk-taking requires that you move through a fear. Do it anyway and you'll gain bravery, confidence and pride each time you step through a fear.

Declare: I feel wonderful every time I overcome a fear.

Safety

Why am I a dare devil?

You might have a thrill-seeking gene called MAO which drives you to experience rushes.

If thrill-seeking is your thing, you get to decide if you do it safely or not. People who care about you will warn you to stay safe.

Declare: I weigh the pros and cons of my behavior to remain safe.

Second Chance

Does everyone deserve a second chance?

Someone has just shown you who he/she was. If the issue is a deal-breaker, one strike, you're out. If it is minor, tell them how important this issue is to you and give them one warning. They snooze, they loose.

Declare: I deserve to be treated with respect. Either you treat me with respect or I shall find someone who will.

Self-Care

Isn't it selfish to care of myself first?

That is a lie you were taught. The *best* thing you can do for others is to care for yourself first. You need to be healthy, strong, rested, fulfilled, and balanced. You can't give what you don't have.

When you are told, "You are being selfish." That may translate to, "You are not doing what I want you to do now so you change."

Declare: I fill myself first so I can give at the highest level to those around me.

Self-Understanding

I don't know who I really am. How can I find out?

Ask yourself, "What matters to me? What are my dreams?" "What am I here to give? What are my talents/ what are my values?"

Read Barbara Sher's book, *Live the Life you Love* then do the exercises she suggests.

Read my book, *Get Unstuck Live with Ease* – find "Values" page and do the exercise.

Declare: I learn something new about me every day. I'm fascinating.

Songs

I love to sing but have a lousy voice. What should I do?

Sing, sing, and sing! Sing in church. Sing while exercising. Sing while cooking. Sing in the shower.

If you want to sing with others, ask a choir director to evaluate your voice. You may have a good voice. If not, you can take singing lessons.

Declare: I sing because I am happy.

Trust

Can I ever learn to trust?

Trust, like any muscle, needs to be exercised to get strong. If you are fearful, you have practiced being afraid.

Take baby steps. Trust your body to work perfectly. Your heart knows when to pump and your lungs know when to inhale and exhale, your eyes know when to blink. You are already trusting. Pay attention to all the ways you already trust and see how quickly you can build more trust. Trust your instincts. You are always right.

Declare: I trust my intuition. I know when and whom to trust.

Trusting after Betrayal

If people betray me, how can I trust them?

Believe them, when someone shows you who they are.

The blessing of betrayal is that it drives you inward where God dwells. That is the most powerful place to be.

Declare: I trust God within and I trust myself. I never let myself down.

Unity

What's the big deal about being in agreement?

When you are locked into being "right," you force others to believe with you or against you. Whatever you push against wears you out.

Being in harmony and accord not only feels better, it is energizing.

Stand for what is right for you, while being willing to understand and listen to what is right for others.

Declare: Co-creating is exciting, delightful and strengthens bonds between people.

Vacation

I can't afford a fancy vacation, so why even take vacation time?

Any break from your routine is a vacation, where you rest and change what you usually do.

You can create picnics in your home, yard, or across town. Try a new restaurant. You can borrow videos, make popcorn, and watch 5 movies in a row. You can swap houses with a friend. Be creative and enjoy yourself so you feel refreshed and energized.

Declare: I can create a fun vacation by changing my environment and routine.

Volunteer

I don't want to volunteer. Is that selfish or wrong?

Do what feels right for you. There is an old saying, "Don't knock it 'til you try it." You may find great satisfaction from helping others.

Giving without expecting pay is a privilege. Givers say their satisfaction is worth far more than they gave.

Declare: It is my privilege to give service as a volunteer.

Weight

Why can't I lose weight?

If you have ruled out medical reasons, and what you have tried has not worked, do something different. Your body is worth taking care of.

Why are you eating? Ask yourself, "What am I really hungry for?" It isn't food.

Eat what you need rather than what you want. Learn from people who are healthy and trim.

Declare: I eat what I need, not what I want.

Wisdom

Why do I do stupid things?

You are distracted, unfocused, and made poor choices because:

1. You wanted to stop discomfort.

2. You feared not having something.

3. You didn't gather enough information – didn't consider the consequences or outcome.

4. You wanted to please someone.

5. No one showed you how to make wise decisions.

Declare: I focus on what I'm doing in the moment.

Work Relationships

Why can't we all get along?

Intelligent creatures control their environments. Some mark territories; some dominate others.

Humans control their personal environments including clothing, household items, and entertainment. When lots of people share space, control issues may arise. Mix in the fact that some never learned to play well with others, so there may be conflict.

Learn basic negotiation skills to get what you want. If someone irritates you, think, "Bless you, be you comforted." Watch for a change because it will happen.

Declare: I get along well and am comfortable in a group.

World Peace

Why don't we have world peace?

World peace begins with each individual. You must first learn to be peaceful within yourself, within your family, work, school, community, country, and then the world.

You are responsible for your part in creating the world you want to live in.

Declare: I will see world peace within my lifetime.

Questions Asked By My Students

Why do I struggle in my spiritual life?

"Struggle" implies resistance or not meeting an expected picture of what a perfect spiritual life looks like.

Spiritual like social relationships take time to develop – the advantage is that God is never going to dump you nor let you down. You might turn away from God or let yourself down. God's love always flows and He's got your back.

Why does it feel like God is toying with me?

When people in our lives manipulate us, we think God does the same. Not so. Whatever you experience is a gift for you to stretch and grow into your best self – no toying is going on.

Why does it seem like God won't answer?

God always answers – the answer may be "Not yet." I look back at some of my prayers and am grateful they were not answered, because I wasn't mature enough to handle them. Ask yourself, "What do I need to know or do in order to receive my answer?"

Why does it feel like God wants a lot more than I can give before he can answer my prayers?

Perhaps God is stretching you into more of your authentic self so you will be prepared to receive your answer.

How do I catch up with my children's lives for the time I have missed and can I make up for all this?

Children are forgiving and resilient. Be honest and sincere with them. Apologize for being absent and tell them you will make it up to them by loving them from this day forward and you will always be there to guild and protect them. Just keep your word and things will be fine.

Why do the guards and staff (not all but most) treat us prisoners like second rate citizens?

We speak the way we were spoken to. If staff or guards were treated disrespectfully, that is all they know. It is not about you so don't take it personally. If they knew better they would do better. Don't let anyone pull you down to their level. Be an example of respect for others . . . no matter what.

Why do I feel more pain for the loss of others than when I'm hurting?

Perhaps you were not allowed to show hurt for yourself so you tuned off that part of your feelings. It is still present and you can open the door whenever you are ready.

How do I strengthen my faith in God? I believe and love Him, however I feel my faith is not where it should be.

Relax into the stillness and feel the loving arms of God surround you, cradling you, rocking you. God is the pulse of your own heart beat – I am, I am, I am. With your hands at your sides, bend your elbows and raise your hands palms away from you. Close your eyes and feel the tingle of God's love in your hands. Talk to God, ask questions, and begin to notice if you can hear the voice of God speak to you. Then follow any direction you receive from God.

Can I truly become a better husband, father and leader to my family or will I default to my old self?

You WILL become a better husband, father and leader to your family. You have already decided and each minute of each day, in the present moment, you can choose thoughts and behaviors that support your decision. It is a choice by choice plan.

Why does God seem to give us more than we can handle constantly?

I have found that when I ask God for help, it is there – sometimes through another person, an idea, more information, letting go of an old belief, or simply the notion that I deserve to struggle NO more.

Is it right to fear God and be excited at the same time?

Fear and excitement have exactly the same physiological sensations in the body. It makes sense that there might be confusion of the two. Ask yourself what you fear about God. Do you see God as all loving, or judgmental and condemning? If you see God as all loving then there's nothing to fear. However, if you believe God to be judgmental then remember God forgives and so can you.

Will I be able to turn my life into a successful or meaningful one?

Absolutely! You have what it takes and I believe in you. Remember each day brings forth a new opportunity for change, and you can become whatever you set your heart and mind to.

Will my case be overturned?

Only God knows. Whatever happens, you are going to be okay.

Will my daughter love me when she grows up?

If you connect with her now, tell her the truth, ask forgiveness and do whatever you can to have a loving relationship with her. More than anything a daughter needs a dad to say, you are beautiful, I'm proud of you, I love you and I've got your back . . . . no matter what.

Is there help for a man that has had a problem respecting women? Not abusing, just putting them on the same level?

Yes there is help. Being aware of it and telling yourself the truth about your behavior is great. Learn to respect yourself first and treat yourself with dignity, kindness and compassion, and then treat everyone else the same way.

What can you do to avoid taking your anger out on people who know you are a Christian, for the wrong they have done to you?

If someone has hurt you, it is natural to be upset. Learning new tools to handle anger in a healthy, safe way will spare you and those around you unhappiness.

As a Christian,, how can I control bad thoughts I have?

I say thoughts are simply thoughts. The best way to clean out unhealthy thoughts is to flush your mind with healthy thoughts. Picture a jar filled with mud. If you run fresh water into it, it washes away the mud so only fresh water is left. The mind is the same way – we add what we want and that flushes out what we don't want.

What is going on with my fiancé and our relationship?

When in jail, it is scary not to be able to control your relationships. Trust that all is well.

Has she been with anyone else?

If she has been with some else, that demonstrates the level of her commitment to the relationship. It isn't about you. If she cannot wait, she isn't right for you, and God has someone better in mind for you.

When will I leave jail?

When you are ready and the authorities believe you are ready to go back out into the world environment.

Will I find a job and a home and go to college?

You can have it all.

Will I ever have a child with a woman of my own seed?

If it is meant to be you will.

Will I win my appeal and clear my name?

I hope so. You will be okay no matter what happens.

Do you believe Jesus Christ is the son of God?

I believe Jesus was the son of God, as are you. God is your heavenly father.

Is there a difference between religion and spirituality?

Religion is a set of doctrines and rules created by man. Spirituality is your personal relationship with God. You then become an expression of the Divine, blessing everyone and everything you encounter.

What happens when you die?

The spirit within each of us lives on forever. Many books have been written giving accounts from people who have experienced dying, or being in coma, then returning to life, where their spirit re-enters their body. It has been substantiated that death is not the end. Death is a transition from one dimension to another, just as birth is a transition. Death as graduating to the next experience.

When I die will I go to hell for my mistakes?

You have already lived in hell while you were on earth. Moving on after death brings you back to God. In God's realm, there is only love.

Acknowledgements

No project is a solitary effort. I thank those closest to me who exhibit abiding, unbridled love - my children, Patricia Young, Amanda Van Valkenburgh, and David Van Valkenburgh and their mates, Steve Young and Kristin Van Valkenburgh.

A special thanks to my grandsons. Daniel Young shared his artistic talent by creating this book cover and Josh Young used his math talent to calculate percentages and averages of changes in students, then created graphs and charts to illustrate these changes. Every accomplishment multiplies and blesses our family in new and wonderful ways.

My deep gratitude to my publisher and friend, Sharon Lund who believes in me, my precious friend, Dottie Bork, who not only gets who I am, but used her keen editorial skills to edit this manuscript, Phyllis Dumont, whose suggestions moved this along, and to my dear friends for their words of encouragement and for cheering me on: Irene Tsatsui, Martha Scott, Mark and Kathy Stern, Tonya Gustafson, Mary Jo Costello, JoAnn Woods, Al Kowahl, Mike Schwager and Dean Short.

Thank you to Reverend Blair Tabor, and Pastor Joel Osteen, whose inspiration keeps me filled and refreshed.

My deep appreciation to all the brave inmates who have been willing to look at their lives, decide what changes they wanted to make, and then had the courage to learn new tools to make those changes possible. I salute you and thank you for allowing me to walk with you on your path and serve you.

About the Author

Judy Winkler

Judy is a retired minister who coaches and counsels clients. She teaches in prisons, including the Miramar Brig and Juvenile Hall, where she observes dramatic life changes.

Judy is the author of *Get Unstuck: Live with Ease.*

Judy lives in San Diego, California and can be reached through her websites:

Coachjudywinkler.com

Revjudywinkler.com